PRAXIS 5004 Social Studies Elementary Education Exam

By: LQ Publications

This page is intentionally left blank.

This page is intentionally left blank.

Free Online Email Tutoring Services

All preparation guides purchased directly from LQ Publications includes a free four months email tutoring subscription. Any resale of preparation guides does not qualify for a free email tutoring subscription.

What is Email Tutoring?

Email Tutoring allows buyers to send questions to tutors via email. Buyers can send any questions regarding the exam processes, strategies, content questions, or practice questions.

LQ Publications reserves the right not to answer questions with or without reason(s).

How to use Email Tutoring?

Buyers need to send an email to lqpublicationgroup@gmail.com requesting email tutoring services. Buyers may be required to confirm the email address used to purchase the preparation guide or additional information prior to using email tutoring. Once email tutoring subscription is confirmed, buyers will be provided an email address to send questions to. The four months period will start the day the subscription is confirmed.

Any misuse of email tutoring services will result in termination of services. LQ Publications reserves the right to terminate email tutoring subscription at anytime with or without notice.

Comments and Suggestions

All comments and suggestions for improvements for the study guide and email tutoring services can be sent to lqpublicationgroup@gmail.com.

This page is intentionally left blank.

Table of Content

This page is intentionally left blank.

About the Exam and Study Guide

About the PRAXIS 5004 Elementary Education Social Studies Exam

The PRAXIS 5004 Elementary Education Exam is a test to measure individuals' knowledge related to social studies topics introduced in Grades K-6. The exam is aligned to national standards and the Common Core State Standards, and the exam covers the following subject areas:

- United States History
- Government and Citizenship
- Geography, Anthropology, and Sociology
- World History
- Economics

The exam consists of 60 selected-response questions, and it is timed at 60 minutes. The exam questions and information are based on material typically covered in college programs related to elementary education.

What is included in this study guide book?

This guide includes two full-length practice tests for the PRAXIS 5004 Elementary Education Exam, along with detailed explanations to each question.

All preparation guides purchased directly from LQ Publications includes a free four months email tutoring subscription. Any resale of preparation guides does not qualify for a free email tutoring subscription.

What is Email Tutoring?

Email Tutoring allows buyers to send questions to tutors via email. Buyers can send any questions regarding the exam processes, strategies, content questions, or practice questions.

How to use Email Tutoring?

Buyers need to send an email to lqpublicationgroup@gmail.com requesting email tutoring services. Buyers may be required to confirm the email address used to purchase the preparation guide or additional information prior to using email tutoring. Once email tutoring subscription is confirmed, buyers will be provided an email address to send questions to. The four months period will start the day the subscription is confirmed.

This page is intentionally left blank.

PRACTICE EXAM 1

This page is intentionally left blank.

Test 1 - Answer Sheet

Question Numbers	Selected Answer	Question Numbers	Selected Answer
1		31	
2		32	
3		33	
4		34	
5		35	
6		36	
7		37	
8		38	
9		39	
10		40	
11		41	
12		42	
13		43	
14		44	
15		45	
16		46	
17		47	
18		48	
19		49	
20		50	
21		51	
22		52	
23		53	
24		54	
25		55	
26		56	
27		57	
28		58	
29		59	
30		60	

This page is intentionally left blank.

Test 1 - Full Practice Exam Questions

QUESTION 1

In an absolute monarchy, control power is given to the king or the queen. Which of the following best indicates who controls power in a democracy?

   A. Grand Old Party
   B. the People
   C. the President
   D. House of Representatives

Answer:

QUESTION 2

Mount Kilimanjaro is located on which continent?

   A. Africa
   B. North America
   C. South America
   D. Asia

Answer:

QUESTION 3

Marbury v. Madison (1803) had a significant impact on American history as it expanded the Supreme Court's power by

   A. establishing the power of judicial review.
   B. establishing the separation of power.
   C. restricting the use of the interstate commerce clause.
   D. providing an interpretation of unconstitutional acts.

Answer:

QUESTION 4

_____ was the first permanent settlement in English North America.

    A. Jamestown

    B. Plymouth

    C. Virginia Colony

    D. Salem Colony

Answer:

QUESTION 5

Of the following, which is not a reason why the Spanish were able to conquer Native American populations?

    A. Sophisticated, strong weapons such as steel swords, crossbows, and guns helped the Spanish against local people, who had less powerful weaponry.

    B. The Spanish conquistadors also had horses, which people in the Americas had never seen before.

    C. Stronger immune system; European explorers carried over several diseases that Native Americans had never encountered before. One such disease was smallpox.

    D. The Spanish conquistadors had significant in-classroom training and field training related to military operations.

Answer:

QUESTION 6

    I.   Thomas Paine

    II.   George Washington

    III.   Paul Revere

    1. _____ led the Continental Army.

    2. _____ wrote Common Sense.

    3. _____ warned the colonists that the British were coming.

Which of the following accurately matches the individuals with the descriptions?

    1 2 3

  A. I, II, III

  B. II, I, III

  C. III, I, II

  D. I, III, II

Answer:

QUESTION 7

Which of the following statement is NOT something an anti-federalist would have said to support the Constitution?

  A. The Constitution indicates federal laws are "the law of the land," so the federal government could just take absolute control.

  B. If the Constitution establishes the President, then the idea is the same as a king.

  C. The United States is too big to have a central government.

  D. The Constitution ensures citizens a role in government.

Answer:

QUESTION 8

Which President served more than two terms?

    A. Theodore Roosevelt

    B. Herbert Hoover

    C. Franklin D. Roosevelt

    D. Ronald Reagan

Answer:

QUESTION 9

Which of the following is NOT a cause of the French and Indian War?

    A. France and Britain armed Native Americans.

    B. France built a fort to keep the British out.

    C. British colonists moved into Ohio River Valley.

    D. Colonists became angry.

Answer:

QUESTION 10

Which of the following reopened the issue of slavery in the areas closed to slavery north of the 36~30' line of the Missouri Compromise?

    A. Fugitive Slave Act

    B. 13th Amendment

    C. Kansas-Nebraska Act of 1854

    D. Three-Fifth Compromise

Answer:

QUESTION 11

Which of the following is NOT a cause of World War I?

    A. The growth of American power in Central Europe challenged the Great Powers (France, Great Britain, Russia).

    B. International competition among European powers for colonies and economic markets.

    C. The naval rivalry between Great Britain and Germany

    D. Breakdown of the European treaty system.

Answer:

QUESTION 12

Which of the following signified the Ottoman Empire was a preeminent power in southeastern Europe and the eastern Mediterranean?

    A. Ottoman conquest of Constantinople in 1453

    B. controlling all former Byzantine lands

    C. capture of Bayezid I

    D. increase revenue and military weapons

Answer:

QUESTION 13

Which of the following was NOT a part of the First New Deal by Franklin D. Roosevelt?

    A. Federal Emergency Relief Act

    B. Agricultural Adjustment Act

    C. Glass-Steagall Act

    D. Social Security Act

Answer:

QUESTION 14

- abdication of Czar Nicholas II
- failure of provisional government
- growing power of the Soviets
- Lenin's return to Russia
- Bolshevik takeover under Lenin

The above best indicates which of the following revolutions?

    A. Russian Revolutions of 1917

    B. The Athenian Revolution

    C. The Ionian Revolt

    D. Lenin Revolutions of 1917

Answer:

QUESTION 15

The Truman Doctrine and the Marshall Plan were examples of which of the following?

    A. restriction policy

    B. containment policy

    C. communist ideology

    D. the arms race

Answer:

QUESTION 16

During the 1950s, American women were expected to _____.

    A. earn money to support their family

    B. obtain college education

    C. work at home and raise children

    D. serve their husbands

Answer:

QUESTION 17

During the Montgomery Bus Boycott, African American citizens

    A. deprived the city bus system of regular passengers.
    B. hindered white citizens from using the city bus system.
    C. joined forces with Rosa Parks in her actions.
    D. formed the Committee on Civil Rights to help cities stage similar boycotts

Answer:

QUESTION 18

Which president's ideology is most associated with the statement, "The Government is not the solution to our problem. Government is the problem?"

    A. Robert Kennedy
    B. Ronald Reagan
    C. Jimmy Carter
    D. Richard Nixon

Answer:

QUESTION 19

The Articles of Confederation gave the states

    A. more power than the national government.
    B. equal powers to the national government.
    C. less power than the national government.
    D. all the power.

Answer:

QUESTION 20

Which of the following is NOT a requirement to vote in the United States elections?

    A. U.S. citizenship
    B. at least 18 years old
    C. registered to vote by the state's voter registration deadline
    D. proof of membership in a political party

Answer:

QUESTION 21

Which of the following states had the highest voter turnout in the 2016 Presidential Election?

    A. Texas
    B. Pennsylvania
    C. Ohio
    D. Michigan

Answer:

QUESTION 22

Which of the following wars was NOT fought by the United States in the 1800s?

    A. Civil War
    B. Spanish-American War
    C. World War I
    D. Mexican-American War

Answer:

QUESTION 23

American Indians used the resources of mud, stones, animal skins, and wood to make which of the following?

A. homes
B. clothes
C. plates
D. rivers

Answer:

QUESTION 24

In the above image, the dotted line indicates which of the following rivers?

A. Mississippi
B. Ohio
C. Rio Grande
D. South Park

Answer:

QUESTION 25

Which of the following is NOT a natural resource?

    A. air
    B. water
    C. soil
    D. canopy

Answer:

QUESTION 26

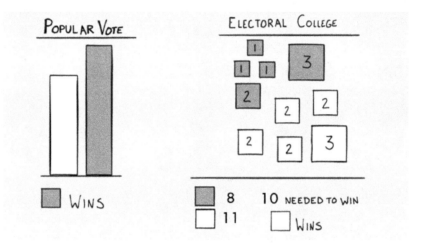

From the above, in presidential elections, which of the following is the most accurate statement?

    A. popular votes do not matter in elections
    B. electoral college does not matter in elections
    C. electoral college will always determine the ultimate winner
    D. electoral college only matters in elections

Answer:

QUESTION 27

Emily's credit was not the best, so she worried about not being able to buy a home.

What is the definition of credit in this sentence?

A. amount of money she owed to others
B. amount of money she had available to use
C. responsibility in paying debt back
D. responsibility for completing an action

Answer:

QUESTION 28

Fill in the blanks accurately.

A _____ is a map that uses differences in shading, coloring, or the placing of symbols within predefined areas to indicate the average values of a property or quantity in those areas while a _____ is a map that emphasizes a particular theme or a special topic such as the average distribution of rainfall in an area.

A. thematic map and topographic map
B. thematic map and choropleth map
C. choropleth map and thematic map
D. topographic map and thematic map

Answer:

QUESTION 29

If the United States disagrees with a foreign country's politics and wants to hinder trading with that country, the best action for the United States to take is to

A. increase safety standards on goods coming from that country.
B. place an embargo on all goods coming from that country.
C. place high tariffs on all goods coming from that country
D. pass laws that hinders goods coming from that country.

Answer:

QUESTION 30

Which region has the most Muslim population?

    A. India
    B. Indonesia
    C. Pakistan
    D. Saudi Arabia

Answer:

QUESTION 31

The dark shading on the map above indicates which of the following climate region?

    A. Desert
    B. Tundra
    C. Highland
    D. Tropical

Answer:

QUESTION 32

Which of the following is the science of making maps?

A. cartography
B. toponymy
C. geomorphology
D. demography

Answer:

QUESTION 33

What is the name of the imaginary line that passes through the North Pole and the South Pole?

A. latitude
B. earth's axis
C. equator
D. earth's axle

Answer:

QUESTION 34

Which of the following is NOT considered a renewable energy resource?

A. coal
B. hydropower
C. wind
D. solar

Answer:

QUESTION 35

Which of the following is NOT considered one of the major social institutions?

    A. religion
    B. economics
    C. community
    D. educational

Answer:

QUESTION 36

Jenny is a sales associate at a local department store. She has been unwilling to help her coworker, Julie, who is newly employed at the department store. When Julie asks a question to Jenny, Jenny ignores her. One day, Jenny needed something from Julie. When Jenny asked Julie, Julie just walked away. Which of the following sociological terms best describes the situation?

    A. negative reinforcement
    B. norm of reciprocity
    C. abuse
    D. unprofessional ethics

Answer:

QUESTION 37

The Statue of Liberty was a joint effort between which two countries?

    A. the United States and Ireland
    B. the United States and Canada
    C. the United States and France
    D. the United States and European Union

Answer:

QUESTION 38

A _____ can best accurately depict true geographical distance, true direction, true shape, and true size.

A. map
B. globe
C. conic projection
D. gnomonic projection

Answer:

QUESTION 39

The Great Mississippi Flood of 1927 and Hurricane Katrina in 2005 are similar because

A. both were as a result of severe hurricanes originating from the Gulf of Mexico.
B. a breach in levees increased the severity of the flooding.
C. it created a long term negative impact on the US economy.
D. the fishing industry never recovered.

Answer:

QUESTION 40

Which of the following actions is an example of an improvement in human capital?

A. Knock's Bakery trains employees to use computers.
B. James hires four workers for his local business.
C. Dallas, TX builds a new recreational facility.
D. Blake applies for a summer internship.

Answer:

QUESTION 41

JJ Local Grocery Store has decided to charge customers for bags. Which of the following is most likely a response to this change?

    A. Customers will shop at other grocery stores.
    B. Customers will buy more goods in bulk.
    C. Customers will exclusively use grocery delivery services.
    D. Customers will visit the store more often.

Answer:

QUESTION 42

Tanja and Marcus made 100 T-shirts with a picture of their school's soccer team to celebrate winning the division championship. They initially sold the T-shirts for $10 each. The T-shirts began selling quickly. Tanja and Marcus realized that $10 a shirt would not cover their costs, so they raised the price to $16 a shirt. As a result, sales declined, and they had 30 unsold T-shirts at the end of the year. Which term best describes what happened when Tanja and Marcus raised the price of the T-shirts?

    A. economic equilibrium
    B. law of supply
    C. law of demand
    D. competition advantage

Answer:

QUESTION 43

Kerry, 14 years old, has inherited $5,000 from his uncle. He wants to invest in an option that has very low risk but still increases the amount of money. He does not plan to access the money until he has completed college. Based on Kerry's requirements, which option would be his best to invest in?

A. stock mark
B. a certificate of deposit
C. saving account
D. gold

Answer:

QUESTION 44

Robin decides to produce and sell orange juice. She leases an orange orchard and renovates her master kitchen to produce and bottle orange juice. Robin hires five employees. Each employee will have a different function in the organization. Robin is best representing which of the following in the manufacture and sale of the orange juice?

A. free market
B. capitalism
C. entrepreneurship
D. success

Answer:

QUESTION 45

What is the most negative aspect of borrowing money from a bank to purchase a car?

A. The car will be worthless in years to come.
B. The car will cost more.
C. The car is paid for over a long period of time.
D. The bank will buy the car when the loan is paid.

Answer:

QUESTION 46

Which source would provide an archaeologist with a primary source of information about pre-Columbian Indians who settled in New York?

    A. an encyclopedia article regarding the Iroquois
    B. an interview with a librarian who specializes in early American cultures
    C. artifacts left by the Iroquois
    D. a newspaper article on pre-Columbian Indians

Answer:

QUESTION 47

Which event caused Britain and France to declare war on Germany in 1939?

    A. invasion of Poland
    B. bombing London
    C. killing of people in Germany
    D. alliance with Soviet Union

Answer:

QUESTION 48

Americans opposed the United States involvement in the war in Vietnam. One reason for this was because

    A. the United States needed to focus on domestic issues.
    B. the conflict should be resolved by the European Union.
    C. the conflict was considered a civil war within the region.
    D. the conflict had no impact on the United States.

Answer:

QUESTION 49

Hindus and Buddhists both share the belief of which of the following?

    A. the law of karma and reincarnation
    B. Jesus Christ is their savior
    C. the Four Noble Truths
    D. caste system

Answer:

QUESTION 50

Which of the following best explains the impact of the Black Plague on Medieval Europe?

    A. It ended the Crusades.
    B. It prompted talks about the global health care system.
    C. It increased birth rates globally within the first year.
    D. It weakened the feudal system.

Answer:

QUESTION 51

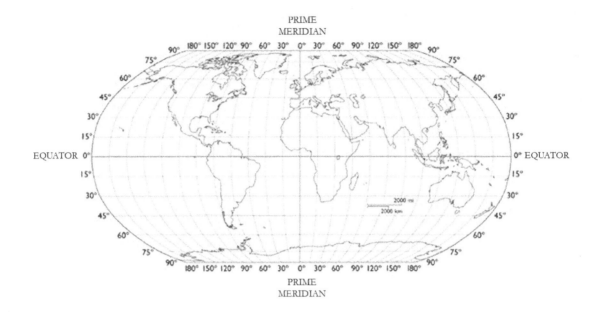

What continent is located at 0°, 60°W?

    A. South America
    B. North America
    C. Antarctica
    D. Africa

Answer:

QUESTION 52

In ancient China, it was easier for rulers to control large areas of land due to _____.

    A. the use of paper money
    B. the existence of transportation resources
    C. the creation of a feudal system
    D. the spread of various religion in the region

Answer:

QUESTION 53

Reasons for Migration

Push factors are no economic prosperity and political unrest.

Pull factors are better jobs and _____.

Which of the following best fills in the blank above?

    A. drought
    B. civil war
    C. healthcare system
    D. religious freedom

Answer:

QUESTION 54

Which of the following early civilization used a simple alphabet as it traded with other individuals?

    A. the Egyptian
    B. the Harrappan
    C. the Phoenician
    D. the Chinese

Answer:

QUESTION 55

Which of the following best describes the relationship between China and the Middle East in the 8th century A.D.?

    A. Both civilizations traded with each other along the Silk Road.

    B. Both civilizations fought a few wars against each other.

    C. Both civilizations practiced the same religion.

    D. Both civilizations had the same cultural traditions.

Answer:

QUESTION 56

    I.   Declaration of Independence

    II.   United States Constitution

    III.   Articles of Confederation

    IV.   Bill of Rights

Which of the following correctly orders the above documents starting from the latest written?

    A. IV, II, III, I

    B. I, II, III, IV

    C. II, III, I, IV

    D. IV, III, II, I

Answer:

QUESTION 57

What is the purpose of celebrating the Fourth of July in the United States?

    A. to honor the new year

    B. to honor past presidents

    C. to honor the birth of the country

    D. to honor the soldiers who died in the American Revolution

Answer:

QUESTION 58

Which of the following states is north of Nebraska?

- A. Missouri
- B. South Dakota
- C. Denver
- D. Mississippi

Answer:

QUESTION 59

Why did Frontier settlers live in log cabins?

- A. used natural materials
- B. were fireproof
- C. weatherproof
- D. had many rooms

Answer:

QUESTION 60

Naturalized citizens cannot run for which two elected offices?

- A. Senator
- B. Governor
- C. Vice President
- D. President

Answer:

This page is intentionally left blank.

Test 1 – Answer Key

Question Numbers	Correct Answer	Question Numbers	Correct Answer
1	B	31	B
2	A	32	A
3	A	33	B
4	A	34	A
5	D	35	C
6	B	36	B
7	D	37	C
8	C	38	B
9	D	39	B
10	C	40	A
11	A	41	A
12	A	42	C
13	D	43	B
14	A	44	C
15	B	45	B
16	C	46	C
17	A	47	A
18	B	48	C
19	A	49	A
20	D	50	D
21	A	51	A
22	C	52	C
23	A	53	D
24	C	54	C
25	D	55	A
26	C	56	A
27	C	57	C
28	C	58	B
29	B	59	A
30	B	60	C and D

NOTE: Getting approximately 80% of the questions correct increases chances of obtaining passing score on the real exam. This varies from different states and university programs.

This page is intentionally left blank.

Test 1 - Full Practice Exam Questions and Explanations

QUESTION 1

In an absolute monarchy, control power is given to the king or the queen. Which of the following best indicates who controls power in a democracy?

    A. Grand Old Party

    B. the People

    C. the President

    D. House of Representatives

Answer: B

Explanation: The controlling power in a democratic system is given to the people. The people vote individuals into offices.

QUESTION 2

Mount Kilimanjaro is located on which continent?

    A. Africa

    B. North America

    C. South America

    D. Asia

Answer: A

Explanation: Mount Kilimanjaro is located in Africa.

QUESTION 3

Marbury v. Madison (1803) had a significant impact on American history as it expanded the Supreme Court's power by

A. establishing the power of judicial review.
B. establishing the separation of power.
C. restricting the use of the interstate commerce clause.
D. providing an interpretation of unconstitutional acts.

Answer: A

Explanation: In Marbury v. Madison, the Supreme Court established the principle of judicial review in which the courts have the power to strike down laws, statutes, and some government actions that contradict with the United States Constitution.

QUESTION 4

_____ was the first permanent settlement in English North America.

A. Jamestown
B. Plymouth
C. Virginia Colony
D. Salem Colony

Answer: A

Explanation: Jamestown was the first permanent settlement in English North America.

QUESTION 5

Of the following, which is not a reason why the Spanish were able to conquer Native American populations?

    A. Sophisticated, strong weapons such as steel swords, crossbows, and guns helped the Spanish against local people, who had less powerful weaponry.
    B. The Spanish conquistadors also had horses, which people in the Americas had never seen before.
    C. Stronger immune system; European explorers carried over several diseases that Native Americans had never encountered before. One such disease was smallpox.
    D. The Spanish conquistadors had significant in-classroom training and field training related to military operations.

Answer: D

Explanation: Historical evidences indicate that stronger weapons, horses, and immune systems contributed to the Spanish being able to conquer Native American populations. No evidence exists of Spanish conquistadors having significant in-classroom training and field training related to military operations.

QUESTION 6

    I.   Thomas Paine

    II.   George Washington

   III.   Paul Revere

    1. _____ led the Continental Army.

    2. _____ wrote Common Sense.

    3. _____ warned the colonists that the British were coming.

Which of the following accurately matches the individuals with the descriptions?

      1 2 3

   A. I, II, III

   B. II, I, III

   C. III, I, II

   D. I, III, II

Answer: B

Explanation: George Washington led the Continental Army. Thomas Paine wrote the Common Sense. Paul Revere warned the colonists that the British were coming.

QUESTION 7

Which of the following statement is NOT something an anti-federalist would have said to support the Constitution?

A. The Constitution indicates federal laws are "the law of the land," so the federal government could just take absolute control.

B. If the Constitution establishes the President, then the idea is the same as a king.

C. The United States is too big to have a central government.

D. The Constitution ensures citizens a role in government.

Answer: D

Explanation: Federalists wanted a strong central government while anti-federalists wanted a small government. Option D is a statement that would be made by a federalist as it indicates that citizens are a part of the government.

QUESTION 8

Which President served more than two terms?

A. Theodore Roosevelt

B. Herbert Hoover

C. Franklin D. Roosevelt

D. Ronald Reagan

Answer: C

Explanation: Franklin D. Roosevelt was the only president to serve more than two terms. In 1940, he won the election for his third term. In 1944, he ran again and became the only president to be elected to a fourth term.

QUESTION 9

Which of the following is NOT a cause of the French and Indian War?

A. France and Britain armed Native Americans.

B. France built a fort to keep the British out.

C. British colonists moved into Ohio River Valley.

D. Colonists became angry.

Answer: D

Explanation: French and Indian War was caused by the following:

- France claimed the interior of North America, while British colonists settled along the coast.
- French and British traded for furs with different Native American groups.
- France and Britain armed Native Americans.
- British colonists moved into Ohio River Valley, claimed by France.
- France built a fort to keep the British out.

Colonists became angry was an effect of the French and Indian War.

QUESTION 10

Which of the following reopened the issue of slavery in the areas closed to slavery north of the 36~30' line of the Missouri Compromise?

A. Fugitive Slave Act

B. 13th Amendment

C. Kansas-Nebraska Act of 1854

D. Three-Fifth Compromise

Answer: C

Explanation: Kansas-Nebraska Act of 1854 included the concept of popular sovereignty, which gave residents the right to decide for themselves whether their territories would enter the Union as free or slave states.

QUESTION 11

Which of the following is NOT a cause of World War I?

- A. The growth of American power in Central Europe challenged the Great Powers (France, Great Britain, Russia).
- B. International competition among European powers for colonies and economic markets.
- C. The naval rivalry between Great Britain and Germany.
- D. Breakdown of the European treaty system.

Answer: A

Explanation: The growth of German power in Central Europe challenged the Great Powers was the cause of World War I. Option A indicates "growth of American power," which is incorrect. Option A is not a cause of World War I.

QUESTION 12

Which of the following signified the Ottoman Empire was a preeminent power in southeastern Europe and the eastern Mediterranean?

- A. Ottoman conquest of Constantinople in 1453
- B. controlling all former Byzantine lands
- C. capture of Bayezid I
- D. increase revenue and military weapons

Answer: A

Explanation: The Ottoman conquest of Constantinople in 1453 by Mehmed II paved the status of the Empire as the preeminent power in southeastern Europe and the eastern Mediterranean.

QUESTION 13

Which of the following was NOT a part of the First New Deal by Franklin D. Roosevelt?

- A. Federal Emergency Relief Act
- B. Agricultural Adjustment Act
- C. Glass-Steagall Act
- D. Social Security Act

Answer: D

Explanation: Social Security Act was a part of the Second New Deal as it focused on long-term support for American citizens. It established a trust fund to which workers and employers contributed. At age sixty-five, individuals could retire and collect monthly payments.

QUESTION 14

- abdication of Czar Nicholas II
- failure of provisional government
- growing power of the Soviets
- Lenin's return to Russia
- Bolshevik takeover under Lenin

The above best indicates which of the following revolutions?

- A. Russian Revolutions of 1917
- B. The Athenian Revolution
- C. The Ionian Revolt
- D. Lenin Revolutions of 1917

Answer: A

Explanation: The description indicates the Russian Revolutions of 1917. The Athenian Revolution focused on establishing democracy in Athens. The Ionian Revolt was associated with revolts in Aeolis, Doris, Cyprus, and Caria.

QUESTION 15

The Truman Doctrine and the Marshall Plan were examples of which of the following?

    A. restriction policy

    B. containment policy

    C. communist ideology

    D. the arms race

Answer: B

Explanation: Truman Doctrine established that the United States would provide political, military, and economic assistance to all democratic nations under threat from external or internal authoritarian forces. The purpose of the Marshall Plan was to rebuild the shattered countries of Europe. These were containment efforts to prevent the spread of communism.

QUESTION 16

During the 1950s, American women were expected to _____.

    A. earn money to support their family

    B. obtain college education

    C. work at home and raise children

    D. serve their husbands

Answer: C

Explanation: During the 1950s, American women were expected to work at home and raise children. This was the mindset that most individuals, men, and women, had during those times.

QUESTION 17

During the Montgomery Bus Boycott, African American citizens

    A. deprived the city bus system of regular passengers.
    B. hindered white citizens from using the city bus system.
    C. joined forces with Rosa Parks in her actions.
    D. formed the Committee on Civil Rights to help cities stage similar boycotts.

Answer: A

Explanation: The Montgomery Bus Boycott was a civil-rights protest during which African Americans refused to ride city buses in Montgomery, Alabama. This was to protest segregated seating. The boycott took place from December 5, 1955, to December 20, 1956. Option C is incorrect as not many others took the same action when she took her stand not to give up her seat.

QUESTION 18

Which president's ideology is most associated with the statement, "The Government is not the solution to our problem. Government is the problem?"

    A. Robert Kennedy
    B. Ronald Reagan
    C. Jimmy Carter
    D. Richard Nixon

Answer: B

Explanation: Ronald Reagan argued that the government was not effective in solving social dilemmas. This is why Ronald Reagan gained support from the American people and gained the presidency in 1980.

QUESTION 19

The Articles of Confederation gave the states

    A. more power than the national government.
    B. equal powers to the national government.
    C. less power than the national government.
    D. all the power.

Answer: A

Explanation: Articles of Confederation established the functions of the national government of the United States after it declared independence from Great Britain. The Articles of Confederation gave the states more power than the national government.

QUESTION 20

Which of the following is NOT a requirement to vote in the United States elections?

    A. U.S. citizenship
    B. at least 18 years old
    C. registered to vote by the state's voter registration deadline
    D. proof of membership in a political party

Answer: D

Explanation: The following are required to vote in the United States elections: U.S. citizen, state's residency requirements, 18 years old on or before Election Day, and registered to vote by the state's voter registration deadline.

QUESTION 21

Which of the following states had the highest voter turnout in the 2016 Presidential Election?

    A. Texas
    B. Pennsylvania
    C. Ohio
    D. Michigan

Answer: A

Explanation: This question does not require detailed knowledge of election data. Of the choices, Texas is the most populated State. In fact, Texas's population is nearly double the other options listed. Therefore, a safe conclusion can be made that the State with the highest voter turnout was Texas in the 2016 Presidential Election.

QUESTION 22

Which of the following wars was NOT fought by the United States in the 1800s?

    A. Civil War
    B. Spanish-American War
    C. World War I
    D. Mexican-American War

Answer: C

Explanation: World War I lasted from July 1914 to November 1918.

QUESTION 23

American Indians used the resources of mud, stones, animal skins, and wood to make which of the following?

A. homes
B. clothes
C. plates
D. rivers

Answer: A

Explanation: American Indians used animal skins and plant fibers to make clothes. American Indians used the resources of mud, stones, animal skins, and wood to make homes.

QUESTION 24

In the above image, the dotted line indicates which of the following rivers?

A. Mississippi
B. Ohio
C. Rio Grande
D. South Park

Answer: C

Explanation: Rio Grande forms the border between the United States and Mexico.

QUESTION 25

Which of the following is NOT a natural resource?

    A. air
    B. water
    C. soil
    D. canopy

Answer: D

Explanation: Natural resources are materials or substances such as minerals, forests, water, and fertile land that occur in nature. Of the options, canopy is not considered a natural resource.

QUESTION 26

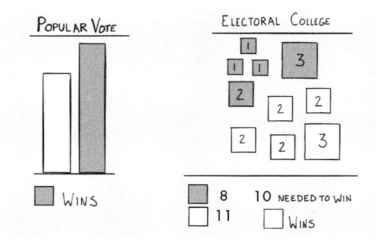

From the above, in presidential elections, which of the following is the most accurate statement?

    A. popular votes do not matter in elections
    B. electoral college does not matter in elections
    C. electoral college will always determine the ultimate winner
    D. electoral college only matters in elections

Answer: C

Explanation: Nothing indicates that popular votes or electoral college do not matter in elections. Option D is incorrect as popular votes do matter in elections. Option C is accurate as the electoral college system will determine the ultimate winner.

QUESTION 27

Emily's credit was not the best, so she worried about not being able to buy a home.

What is the definition of credit in this sentence?

    A. amount of money she owed to others
    B. amount of money she had available to use
    C. responsibility in paying debt back
    D. responsibility for completing an action

Answer: C

Explanation: Credit can have multiple meanings. In this case, it is the responsibility to pay back the debt. Emily has bad credit as she has not paid her debt in a timely manner, which is causing her anxiety about buying a home.

QUESTION 28

Fill in the blanks accurately.

A _____ is a map that uses differences in shading, coloring, or the placing of symbols within predefined areas to indicate the average values of a property or quantity in those areas while a _____ is a map that emphasizes a particular theme or a special topic such as the average distribution of rainfall in an area.

    A. thematic map and topographic map
    B. thematic map and choropleth map
    C. choropleth map and thematic map
    D. topographic map and thematic map

Answer: C

Explanation: A choropleth is a map that uses differences in shading, coloring, or the placing of symbols within predefined areas to indicate the average values of a property or quantity in those selected areas while a thematic is a map that emphasizes a particular theme or a special topic such as the average distribution of rainfall in a selected area. A topographic map is characterized by large-scale detail and quantitative representation of relief, usually using contour lines.

QUESTION 29

If the United States disagrees with a foreign country's politics and wants to hinder trading with that country, the best action for the United States to take is to

    A. increase safety standards on goods coming from that country.
    B. place an embargo on all goods coming from that country.
    C. place high tariffs on all goods coming from that country.
    D. pass laws that hinders goods coming from that country.

Answer: B

Explanation: The best approach is to put an embargo on all goods from that country as all trade will have to stop. This will show a strong stand that the foreign country's politics are unacceptable.

QUESTION 30

Which region has the most Muslim population?

    A. India
    B. Indonesia
    C. Pakistan
    D. Saudi Arabia

Answer: B

Explanation: The keyword in the question is "most." The largest Muslim population is in Indonesia, a nation home to ~12.7% of the world's Muslims, followed by Pakistan and India.

QUESTION 31

The dark shading on the map above indicates which of the following climate region?

    A. Desert
    B. Tundra
    C. Highland
    D. Tropical

Answer: B

Explanation: The tundra is located at the top of the world, near the North Pole. Parts of Alaska and the countries of Canada, Greenland, Iceland, Norway, and Russia are included in the Arctic tundra biome. In the map above, parts of Canada and Greenland are included in the shaded region.

QUESTION 32

Which of the following is the science of making maps?

    A. cartography
    B. toponymy
    C. geomorphology
    D. demography

Answer: A

Explanation: The making of maps is considered cartography. Toponymy is the study of place names. Geomorphology is the study of the physical features of the surface of the earth and their relation to its geological structures. Demography is the study of statistics such as births, deaths, income, or the incidence of disease.

QUESTION 33

What is the name of the imaginary line that passes through the North Pole and the South Pole?

    A. latitude
    B. earth's axis
    C. equator
    D. earth's axle

Answer: B

Explanation: Earth's axis is the imaginary line that passes through the North Pole and the South Pole.

QUESTION 34

Which of the following is NOT considered a renewable energy resource?

    A. coal
    B. hydropower
    C. wind
    D. solar

Answer: A

Explanation: Coal is considered a nonrenewable energy resource as the supply availability is limited.

QUESTION 35

Which of the following is NOT considered one of the major social institutions?

    A. religion
    B. economics
    C. community
    D. educational

Answer: C

Explanation: Five major institutions in rural sociology are political, educational, economic, family, and religion.

QUESTION 36

Jenny is a sales associate at a local department store. She has been unwilling to help her coworker, Julie, who is newly employed at the department store. When Julie asks a question to Jenny, Jenny ignores her. One day, Jenny needed something from Julie. When Jenny asked Julie, Julie just walked away. Which of the following sociological terms best describes the situation?

    A. negative reinforcement
    B. norm of reciprocity
    C. abuse
    D. unprofessional ethics

Answer: B

Explanation: The norm of reciprocity requires that we repay in kind what another has done for us. Jenny was mean to Julie, so Julie undertook the same approach.

QUESTION 37

The Statue of Liberty was a joint effort between which two countries?

    A. the United States and Ireland
    B. the United States and Canada
    C. the United States and France
    D. the United States and European Union

Answer: C

Explanation: The Statue of Liberty was a joint effort between France and the United States, intended to commemorate the lasting friendship between the peoples of the two nations.

QUESTION 38

A _____ can best accurately depict true geographical distance, true direction, true shape, and true size.

A. map
B. globe
C. conic projection
D. gnomonic projection

Answer: B

Explanation: Globe is the only option that can best accurately depict true geographical distance, true direction, true shape, and true size.

QUESTION 39

The Great Mississippi Flood of 1927 and Hurricane Katrina in 2005 are similar because

A. both were as a result of severe hurricanes originating from the Gulf of Mexico.
B. a breach in levees increased the severity of the flooding.
C. it created a long term negative impact on the US economy.
D. the fishing industry never recovered.

Answer: B

Explanation: In both events, the levee system's failure was the primary cause of the extensive flooding. Floodwalls started breaching due to faulty design and inadequate construction.

QUESTION 40

Which of the following actions is an example of an improvement in human capital?

    A. Knock's Bakery trains employees to use computers.
    B. James hires four workers for his local business.
    C. Dallas, TX builds a new recreational facility.
    D. Blake applies for a summer internship.

Answer: A

Explanation: Human capital is mainly dealing with investing in humans (employees). Option A is the best option that shows improvement in human capital. Employees are learning to use computers, which is a development in their skills.

QUESTION 41

JJ Local Grocery Store has decided to charge customers for bags. Which of the following is most likely a response to this change?

    A. Customers will shop at other grocery stores.
    B. Customers will buy more goods in bulk.
    C. Customers will exclusively use grocery delivery services.
    D. Customers will visit the store more often.

Answer: A

Explanation: Due to the extra charge on bags, individuals will go elsewhere to buy groceries. All the other options are possible but unlikely. The best answer is Option A.

QUESTION 42

Tanja and Marcus made 100 T-shirts with a picture of their school's soccer team to celebrate winning the division championship. They initially sold the T-shirts for $10 each. The T-shirts began selling quickly. Tanja and Marcus realized that $10 a shirt would not cover their costs, so they raised the price to $16 a shirt. As a result, sales declined, and they had 30 unsold T-shirts at the end of the year. Which term best describes what happened when Tanja and Marcus raised the price of the T-shirts?

    A. economic equilibrium
    B. law of supply
    C. law of demand
    D. competition advantage

Answer: C

Explanation: If an item has a low price, consumers will buy more of the item than if the price is high. If the price of an item increases, the consumer demand for that item decreases.

QUESTION 43

Kerry, 14 years old, has inherited $5,000 from his uncle. He wants to invest in an option that has very low risk but still increases the amount of money. He does not plan to access the money until he has completed college. Based on Kerry's requirements, which option would be his best to invest in?

    A. stock mark
    B. a certificate of deposit
    C. saving account
    D. gold

Answer: B

Explanation: Wanting a low-risk investment and no desire to access the money, the best option is a certificate of deposit. A certificate of deposit will give him a return on his money with very low risk. Not accessing the money for sometime will allow the bank to give him a higher rate of return.

QUESTION 44

Robin decides to produce and sell orange juice. She leases an orange orchard and renovates her master kitchen to produce and bottle orange juice. Robin hires five employees. Each employee will have a different function in the organization. Robin is best representing which of the following in the manufacture and sale of the orange juice?

   A. free market
   B. capitalism
   C. entrepreneurship
   D. success

Answer: C

Explanation: The keyword here is "best." Of the option, entrepreneurship is the best answer. Robin is the entrepreneur who takes steps to start and to maintain a business.

QUESTION 45

What is the most negative aspect of borrowing money from a bank to purchase a car?

   A. The car will be worthless in years to come.
   B. The car will cost more.
   C. The car is paid for over a long period of time.
   D. The bank will buy the car when the loan is paid.

Answer: B

Explanation: When borrowing money from a bank, there is interest associated with the loan. As a result, the car will cost more, which is the most negative aspect of borrowing money. Option C is incorrect as someone can immediately pay the full loan at any time, depending on the terms of the loan. Option C is not always true, so that is why Option C is not the answer.

QUESTION 46

Which source would provide an archaeologist with a primary source of information about pre-Columbian Indians who settled in New York?

  A. an encyclopedia article regarding the Iroquois
  B. an interview with a librarian who specializes in early American cultures
  C. artifacts left by the Iroquois
  D. a newspaper article on pre-Columbian Indians

Answer: C

Explanation: The key here is primary source, and the only primary source is Option C. The Iroquois people, which included pre-Columbian Indians, have inhabited the areas of Ontario and upstate New York for well over thousands of years.

QUESTION 47

Which event caused Britain and France to declare war on Germany in 1939?

  A. invasion of Poland
  B. bombing London
  C. killing of people in Germany
  D. alliance with Soviet Union

Answer: A

Explanation: Britain and France were at war with Germany following the invasion of Poland. That was one of the main events that caused Britain and France to declare war on Germany in 1939.

QUESTION 48

Americans opposed the United States involvement in the war in Vietnam. One reason for this was because

- A. the United States needed to focus on domestic issues.
- B. the conflict should be resolved by the European Union.
- C. the conflict was considered a civil war within the region.
- D. the conflict had no impact on the United States.

Answer: C

Explanation: Americans opposed involvement in the war in Vietnam as the conflict was considered a civil war and did not concern the United States.

QUESTION 49

Hindus and Buddhists both share the belief of which of the following?

- A. the law of karma and reincarnation
- B. Jesus Christ is their savior
- C. the Four Noble Truths
- D. caste system

Answer: A

Explanation: Hindus and Buddhists both share the belief in the law of karma and reincarnation.

QUESTION 50

Which of the following best explains the impact of the Black Plague on Medieval Europe?

A. It ended the Crusades.
B. It prompted talks about the global health care system.
C. It increased birth rates globally within the first year.
D. It weakened the feudal system.

Answer: D

Explanation: The Black Plague swept over Europe and wiped out a third of its population, which also caused the feudal system to be weakened.

QUESTION 51

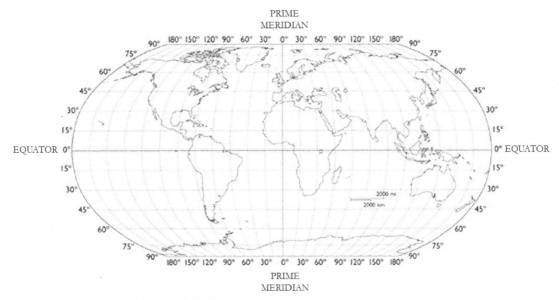

What continent is located at 0°, 60°W?

A. South America
B. North America
C. Antarctica
D. Africa

Answer: A

Explanation: Using the rules of longitude and latitude, the location of 0°, 60°W is South America.

QUESTION 52

In ancient China, it was easier for rulers to control large areas of land due to _____.

    A. the use of paper money
    B. the existence of transportation resources
    C. the creation of a feudal system
    D. the spread of various religion in the region

Answer: C

Explanation: Feudalism was the medieval model of government before the birth of the modern nation-state. A feudal society is a military hierarchy in which a ruler or lord offers a portion of land to control in exchange for military service.

QUESTION 53

Reasons for Migration

Push factors are no economic prosperity and political unrest.

Pull factors are better jobs and _____.

Which of the following best fills in the blank above?

    A. drought
    B. civil war
    C. healthcare system
    D. religious freedom

Answer: D

Explanation: History has shown that one of the reasons for migration is religious freedom.

QUESTION 54

Which of the following early civilization used a simple alphabet as it traded with other individuals?

- A. the Egyptian
- B. the Harrappan
- C. the Phoenician
- D. the Chinese

Answer: C

Explanation: The Phoenician used a simple alphabet as it traded with other people. Phoenician alphabet, writing system that developed out of the North Semitic alphabet, was spread over the Mediterranean area by Phoenician traders.

QUESTION 55

Which of the following best describes the relationship between China and the Middle East in the 8th century A.D.?

- A. Both civilizations traded with each other along the Silk Road.
- B. Both civilizations fought a few wars against each other.
- C. Both civilizations practiced the same religion.
- D. Both civilizations had the same cultural traditions.

Answer: A

Explanation: Chinese and Middle Eastern civilizations traded with each other along the Silk Road.

QUESTION 56

    I.   Declaration of Independence

    II.   United States Constitution

    III.   Articles of Confederation

    IV.   Bill of Rights

Which of the following correctly orders the above documents starting from the latest written?

    A. IV, II, III, I

    B. I, II, III, IV

    C. II, III, I, IV

    D. IV, III, II, I

Answer: A

Explanation: Declaration of Independence was written in 1776. Articles of Confederation came in 1781. The United States Constitution was ratified in 1788. Bill of Rights was ratified in 1791.

QUESTION 57

What is the purpose of celebrating the Fourth of July in the United States?

    A. to honor the new year

    B. to honor past presidents

    C. to honor the birth of the country

    D. to honor the soldiers who died in the American Revolution

Answer: C

Explanation: Independence Day is a federal holiday in the United States celebrating the Declaration of Independence of the United States on July 4, 1776. Fourth of July is to honor the birth of the country.

QUESTION 58

Which of the following states is north of Nebraska?

    A. Missouri

    B. South Dakota

    C. Denver

    D. Mississippi

Answer: B

Explanation: Nebraska is bordered by South Dakota to the north; Colorado to the southwest; Kansas to the south; Iowa to the east and Missouri to the southeast, both across the Missouri River; and Wyoming to the west.

QUESTION 59

Why did Frontier settlers live in log cabins?

    A. used natural materials

    B. were fireproof

    C. weatherproof

    D. had many rooms

Answer: A

Explanation: At the time, Frontier settlers lived in log cabins as the materials used was natural.

QUESTION 60

Naturalized citizens cannot run for which two elected offices?

    A. Senator

    B. Governor

    C. Vice President

    D. President

Answer: C and D

Explanation: In general, naturalized citizens can run for any elected position except that of the President and the Vice President.

This page is intentionally left blank.

PRACTICE EXAM 2

This page is intentionally left blank.

Test 2 – Answer Sheet

Question Numbers	Selected Answer	Question Numbers	Selected Answer
1		31	
2		32	
3		33	
4		34	
5		35	
6		36	
7		37	
8		38	
9		39	
10		40	
11		41	
12		42	
13		43	
14		44	
15		45	
16		46	
17		47	
18		48	
19		49	
20		50	
21		51	
22		52	
23		53	
24		54	
25		55	
26		56	
27		57	
28		58	
29		59	
30		60	

This page is intentionally left blank.

Test 2 - Full Practice Exam Questions

QUESTION 1

Law and order exist mainly due to the existence of which of the following?

- A. democracy
- B. government
- C. political systems
- D. immigration

Answer:

QUESTION 2

Which of the following increased the most as a result of the success in cash crops?

- A. free-market economy
- B. slave trade
- C. land ownership
- D. increase in birth rates

Answer:

QUESTION 3

Which of the following is NOT a motive for European exploration?

- A. crusades
- B. reformation
- C. farms and fortune
- D. advancement in health

Answer:

QUESTION 4

Proclamation of 1763, Quartering Act, Boston Massacre, and Intolerable Acts contributed to which of the following wars?

   A. French and Indian War
   B. American Revolution
   C. War of 1812
   D. Spanish-American War

Answer:

QUESTION 5

Which of the following statement is NOT something a Federalist would have said to support the Constitution?

   A. A robust President is needed to protect the country against foreign attack and make sure laws are carried out properly.
   B. The Supreme Court powers are the weakest as the Supreme Court cannot control the military and be unable to pass laws.
   C. The federal government does not have the power to limit peoples' freedom.
   D. The Constitution provides the federal government enough power to overpower the states.

Answer:

QUESTION 6

Following the ratification of the Constitution of the United States, which of the following actions best displays that the Constitution would not become a new monarch?

   A. The inclusion of the Bill of Rights.
   B. George Washington stepping down after two terms as President.
   C. Vermont being admitted as the 14th State of the United States.
   D. Congress amending the method of electing the President.

Answer:

QUESTION 7

    I.   explore the Missouri River

    II. take observations of latitude & longitude, courses of the river, variations of the compass

    III. observe the soil & face of the country

The above best represents which of the following?

    A. Thomas Jefferson's instructions to Lewis and Clark

    B. agreement with France for Louisiana Territory

    C. exploration of oil and gas offshore in the Gulf of Mexico

    D. Missouri Compromise of 1819

Answer:

QUESTION 8

Which of the following was the main reason British started to tax colonists?

    A. to start building roads

    B. to start community services

    C. to pay the debt of the war

    D. to gain money for government jobs

Answer:

QUESTION 9

The formation of the Republican Party came as a direct passage of which of the following?

    A. Kansas-Nebraska Act

    B. Intolerable Act

    C. the Constitution

    D. the Articles of Confederation

Answer:

QUESTION 10

In the Dred Scott decision of 1857, which act of Congress was declared unconstitutional by the United States Supreme Court?

    A. Fugitive Slave Law

    B. Kansas-Nebraska Act

    C. Missouri Compromise

    D. Commerce Compromise

Answer:

QUESTION 11

Which of the following was NOT a direct cause of the Great Depression?

    A. Bank failure resulted in the loss of uninsured savings.

    B. The American economic policy with Europe.

    C. The stock market crashed on Black Tuesday.

    D. The aftermath of World War II.

Answer:

QUESTION 12

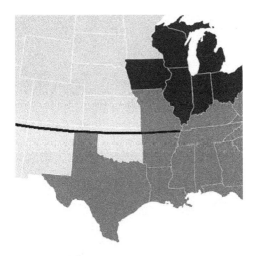

The black line in the image above best represents which of the following?

A. Three-Fifth Compromise

B. Kansas-Nebraska Act

C. Missouri Compromise

D. Commerce Compromise

Answer:

QUESTION 13

Which country was NOT a part of the Triple Alliance?

A. Germany

B. Italy

C. Russia

D. Austria-Hungary

Answer:

QUESTION 14

Which of the following best describes the concentration of the Second New Deal?

    A. relief, recovery, and reform

    B. relief and recovery

    C. recovery and reform

    D. relief and reform

Answer:

QUESTION 15

Which of the following is the long term consequence of the Great Depression?

    A. unemployment

    B. poverty

    C. rise of fascism

    D. deterioration in education systems

Answer:

QUESTION 16

    I.   the fall of Poland

    II.   Lend-Lease Act

    III.   British forces leave Western Europe

    IV.   Allies stranded at Dunkirk

Of the above, which of the following are the causes of World War II?

    A. I and IV

    B. II and IV

    C. I and III

    D. III and IV

Answer:

QUESTION 17

  I. Donald Trump

  II. Herbert Hoover

  III. Dwight Eisenhower

  IV. Zachary Taylor

Which two presidents had neither prior military nor political experiences?

  A. I and II

  B. I and III

  C. I and IV

  D. III and IV

Answer:

QUESTION 18

Which of the following best describes the difference between the League of Nations and the United Nations?

  A. League of Nations did not have members from several of the world's most important industrialized nations.

  B. League of Nations had the authority to enforce decisions made by the World Court.

  C. League of Nations could pass a resolution to intervene in any war.

  D. League of Nations focused on improving world health standards and providing aid to countries involved in wars.

Answer:

QUESTION 19

Which of the following civil rights activists is most closely associated with the first large-scale United States demonstration against segregation?

    A. Rosa Parks
    B. Malcolm X
    C. Harriet Tubman
    D. Emily Dickenson

Answer:

QUESTION 20

When designing the American government, the framers of the Constitution

    A. wanted a strong central government.
    B. rejected the British constitutional tradition.
    C. preferred the French constitution than the British constitution.
    D. wanted all power to be distrusted to the colonies.

Answer:

QUESTION 21

Which of the following was the first to display the concept of supremacy of law over public officials?

    A. Magna Carta
    B. Common Sense
    C. Declaration of Independence
    D. Emancipation Proclamation

Answer:

QUESTION 22

Under the Federal System of Government, which of the following can be done by the state government and not the federal government?

A. set up schools
B. set up a postal service
C. can collect taxes
D. borrow money

Answer:

QUESTION 23

Which of the following amendment does NOT deal with voting?

A. 15th Amendment
B. 16th Amendment
C. 23rd Amendment
D. 46th Amendment

Answer:

QUESTION 24

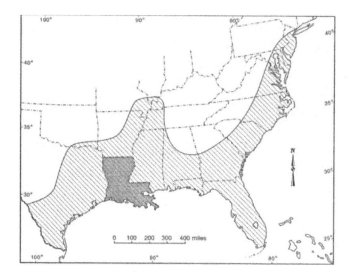

In the above image, what is indicated by the dash lines?

A. Coastal Plain
B. Appalachian Highlands
C. Canadian Shield
D. Interior Lowlands

Answer:

QUESTION 25

During the 20th century, there were fewer farms and fewer framers due to which of the following?

A. advancement in technology
B. expansion of the internet
C. expansion of formal education system
D. decrease in population in rural areas

Answer:

QUESTION 26

In the above image, the dash line area indicates which of the following?

A. Great Plains
B. Interior Lowlands
C. Basin and Range
D. Coastal Range

Answer:

QUESTION 27

Which of the following should be placed in the blank box in the image above?

A. China
B. Kashmir
C. Nepal
D. Bangladesh

Answer:

QUESTION 28

Movement of massive glaciers through the mid-continent, a process that began about one million years ago during the Pleistocene Epoch, resulted in what is known today as _____.

A. Helena Mountains
B. Great Lakes
C. Arctic Blast
D. Greenland

Answer:

QUESTION 29

Pacific – 3:00 ; Mountain – 4:00; Central – 5:00; Eastern – 6:00

A flight leaves Houston, Texas, at 2:00 PM for Riverside, California. The duration of the flight is four and one-half hours. According to the map above, what will be the local time in Riverside when the flight lands?

A. 1:30 PM
B. 4:30 PM
C. 6:30 PM
D. 7:30 PM

Answer:

QUESTION 30

Madison is writing a report about life in modern Pakistan. His teacher asked him to use a primary source and two secondary sources. Which resource could Madison use as a primary source?

    A. the diary of a Pakistani poet
    B. an encyclopedia article about Pakistan
    C. a chapter about Pakistan from his history book
    D. a timeline showing major events in Pakistan history

Answer:

QUESTION 31

What is the name of the imaginary line that divides the Earth into Northern and Southern Hemispheres?

    A. latitude
    B. longitude
    C. equator
    D. prime meridian

Answer:

QUESTION 32

    I. The equator is a line of latitude.
    II. The prime meridian is a line of longitude.
    III. The equator is an imaginary line at 0-degree longitude.

Of the above, which of the statements are accurately written?

    A. I, II, and III
    B. I and II
    C. I and III
    D. II and III

Answer:

QUESTION 33

Which of the following determines a person's job, social group, and marriage?

    A. caste system
    B. hierarchy system
    C. marriage status
    D. societies norm status

Answer:

QUESTION 34

Which of the following best indicates the earliest to latest use of renewable energy resources?

    A. wood – fossil fuels – hydropower – biofuels
    B. fossil fuels – wood – hydropower – biofuels
    C. wood – fossil fuels – biofuels – hydropower
    D. hydropower – biofuels – fossil fuels – wood

Answer:

QUESTION 35

Of the following, which best explains how deviance helps strengthen conformity in society?

    A. It requires no need for agents of social control.
    B. Establishes boundaries between right and wrong.
    C. Establishes punishment for wrongful acts.
    D. It requires people to follow the rules of society.

Answer:

QUESTION 36

Which of the following societies had the greatest impact on modern democratic societies?

    A. Ancient Roman
    B. Ancient Athens
    C. Roman Republic
    D. Byzantine Empire

Answer:

QUESTION 37

All of the following contributed to the War of 1812 except:

    A. The British navy's practice of removing sailors from American merchant ships.
    B. Many in Britain thought that Presidents Jefferson and Madison were pro-French and anti-British.
    C. The American perception that Britain did not recognize her as a fully independent nation.
    D. Britain had been fighting the United States, more or less, since 1793.

Answer:

QUESTION 38

If California experiences a year-long drought, a significant negative effect can be on which of the following?

    A. fruit production
    B. population patterns
    C. tourism
    D. employment

Answer:

QUESTION 39

Which of the following countries is currently at the most economic risk due to a reduction in petroleum resources?

A. Iran
B. Iraq
C. Mexico
D. Venezuela

Answer:

QUESTION 40

Jimmy asked the bank to give him $10,000. By the time the loan is repaid, Jimmy has paid the bank $10,600. What does the additional $600 represent?

A. interest
B. investment
C. fees
D. inflation rate

Answer:

QUESTON 41

Country X has no domestic sources of wood; it imports all wood from wood-producing countries. If the price of wood in wood-producing countries rises substantially, which of the following is most likely to occur?

A. Country X will see a quick decline in home construction.
B. Country X will import more woods to meet rising demand.
C. Country X will use an alternative material to construct homes.
D. Country X will see an increase in housing prices.

Answer:

QUESTION 42

Kelly has decided to give up her part-time job to return to school. Which of the following is one potential economic risk Kelly is accepting?

    A. the loss of income from giving up her part-time job
    B. possibility of not getting a job in the field, Kelly has decided to go back to school for
    C. not finding another part-time job in the future
    D. the increase in expenses due to going back to school

Answer:

QUESTION 43

Which of the following best illustrates the meaning of the economic term scarcity?

    A. individuals unable to buy basic household items
    B. businesses lack funds to invest in making a profit
    C. employees lack of training to gain career advances
    D. manufactures lack raw materials necessary to fulfill demand

Answer:

QUESTION 44

Monopoly is best characterized as

    A. strong control over price.
    B. strong control over items.
    C. rarely influenced by government.
    D. few barriers to reach the market.

Answer:

QUESTION 45

A Alpha	B Beta	Γ Gamma	Δ Delta	E Epsilon	Z Zeta
H Eta	Θ Theta	I Iota	K Kappa	Λ Lambda	M Mu
N Nu	Ξ Xi	O Omicron	Π Pi	P Rho	Σ Sigma
T Tau	Y Upsilon	Φ Phi	X Chi	Ψ Psi	Ω Omega

The above form of writing belongs to which ancient civilization?

A. Sumerian
B. Egyptian
C. Greek
D. Hebrew

Answer:

QUESTION 46

Columbia grows coffee efficiently and effectively, and coffee is the country's largest agricultural product. Columbia also has an automobile industry that is unable to efficiently manufacture automobiles. The United States efficiently manufactures automobiles; however, the country grows a small amount of coffee in Utah. Columbia's economy is ranked below 10th in the world, while the United States has the largest economy. Based on the information, which statement best explains why Columbia would want to trade with the United States?

A. Columbia has a comparative advantage in growing coffee over the United States.
B. Columbia needs more cars in the streets for transportation to support the coffee business.
C. Columbia has a comparative advantage in the technological advantage in the manufacturing of automobiles over the United States.
D. Columbia needs to sell coffee to the United States, or Columbia's economy will not sustain.

Answer:

QUESTION 47

In a market economy, if the price of an item increases, the quantity demand by buyers and quantity supplied by producers will change in which of the following ways?

	Quantity Demanded Quantity	Supplied by Consumers by Producers
A.	decrease	increase
B.	decrease	decrease
C.	increase	increase
D.	increase	decrease

Answer:

QUESTION 48

What is the impact on the United States with increased oil usage around the world?

A. Individuals pay more for gasoline.
B. Energy sales remain the same.
C. Energy cost declines.
D. Individuals' need for gasoline decreases.

Answer:

QUESTION 49

Which of the following organization is responsible for the promotion of consumer protection and the elimination and prevention of anticompetitive business practices?

A. Federal Reserve Bank
B. Federal Trade Commission
C. Consumer Protection Agency
D. United States Commerce Department

Answer:

QUESTION 50

In 2018, California had 53 representatives in the United States House of Representatives while Louisiana had 6 representatives. What accounts for the differences in these numbers?

A. land area of the states
B. population of the states
C. wealth within the states
D. number of counties within the states

Answer:

QUESTION 51

Which of the following best describes the idea of manifest destiny?

A. slavery should be allowed in the East
B. all individuals had the right to freedom
C. preventing European colonies from entering into the Americas
D. the United States had the right to expand to the Pacific Ocean

Answer:

QUESTION 52

Which of the following is an example of a factor of production?

A. supply
B. demand
C. development
D. entrepreneurship

Answer:

QUESTION 53

    I.   high population growth rate/size
    II. high rates of unemployment
    III. high per capita real income

Of the above, which of the following accurately characterizes developing countries?

    A. I and II
    B. I and III
    C. II and III
    D. I, II, and III

Answer:

QUESTION 54

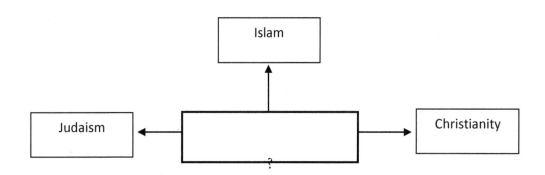

Which of the following best completes the web?

    A. acknowledge the existence of Jesus
    B. use of the same holy book
    C. holy city of Mecca
    D. karma

Answer:

QUESTION 55

What was the main reason why Phoenicians establish dozens of colonies along the Mediterranean coast?

    A. to make money
    B. to protect their main cities from invaders
    C. to improve and expand trade
    D. to attract new members to their civilization

Answer:

QUESTION 56

Which of the following best displays the action of a good citizen?

    A. joining a library club
    B. throwing away litter
    C. buying a new house
    D. making a dinner

Answer:

QUESTION 57

Population and Square Miles of Countries

Country	Land in square miles	Population in millions
Egypt	6500	5.5
Iraq	172344	20.2
Jordan	35343	3.8
Iran	163234	18.5

According to the above data, which country is the most densely populated?

    A. Egypt

    B. Iraq

    C. Jordan

    D. Iran

Answer:

QUESTION 58

Which of the following is a finished product?

    A. laptop

    B. horse

    C. plant

    D. mountain

Answer:

QUESTION 59

Flake wrote a school article about six goods produced in China and sold to other countries. What is the best title for Flake's report?

    A. Jobs in China

    B. Exports of China

    C. Items in China

    D. Buyers in China

Answer:

QUESTION 60

Which region is usually hot, very dry, and has few trees?

    A. arctic

    B. grassland

    C. rain forest

    D. desert

Answer:

This page is intentionally left blank.

Test 2 – Answer Key

Question Numbers	Correct Answer	Question Numbers	Correct Answer
1	B	31	C
2	B	32	B
3	D	33	A
4	B	34	B
5	D	35	B
6	B	36	B
7	A	37	D
8	C	38	A
9	A	39	C
10	C	40	A
11	D	41	D
12	C	42	B
13	C	43	D
14	D	44	A
15	C	45	C
16	B	46	A
17	A	47	A
18	A	48	A
19	A	49	B
20	B	50	B
21	A	51	D
22	A	52	D
23	B	53	A
24	A	54	A
25	A	55	C
26	C	56	B
27	B	57	A
28	B	58	A
29	B	59	B
30	A	60	D

NOTE: Getting approximately 80% of the questions correct increases chances of obtaining passing score on the real exam. This varies from different states and university programs.

This page is intentionally left blank.

Test 2 - Full Practice Exam Questions and Explanations

QUESTION 1

Law and order exist mainly due to the existence of which of the following?

- A. democracy
- B. government
- C. political systems
- D. immigration

Answer: B

Explanation: One of the main purposes of government is to provide law and order.

QUESTION 2

Which of the following increased the most as a result of the success in cash crops?

- A. free-market economy
- B. slave trade
- C. land ownership
- D. increase in birth rates

Answer: B

Explanation: Plantation economies rely on the export of cash crops as a source of income. Prominent crops included cotton, rubber, sugar cane, tobacco, figs, rice, kapok, sisal, and etc. In the process of exporting, labor was required. Slave trade was increased to support the export of cash crops.

QUESTION 3

Which of the following is NOT a motive for European exploration?

- A. crusades
- B. reformation
- C. farms and fortune
- D. advancement in health

Answer: D

Explanation: Crusades, renaissance, reformation, technological advances, fame, and fortunes were motives for European exploration.

QUESTION 4

Proclamation of 1763, Quartering Act, Boston Massacre, and Intolerable Acts contributed to which of the following wars?

- A. French and Indian War
- B. American Revolution
- C. War of 1812
- D. Spanish-American War

Answer: B

Explanation: Proclamation of 1763 ordered colonists not to settle west of the Appalachian Mountains. Quartering Act forced colonists to allow British soldiers to stay in their homes and provide them with supplies needed. Boston Massacre was a disagreement between a group of colonists and British soldiers that led to the colonists throwing ice and snow at the soldiers. Intolerable Acts were a series of laws passed by Parliament to punish the colonists for the Boston Tea Party. These were all causes for the American Revolution.

QUESTION 5

Which of the following statement is NOT something a Federalist would have said to support the Constitution?

    A. A robust President is needed to protect the country against foreign attack and make sure laws are carried out properly.

    B. The Supreme Court powers are the weakest as the Supreme Court cannot control the military and be unable to pass laws.

    C. The federal government does not have the power to limit peoples' freedom.

    D. The Constitution provides the federal government enough power to overpower the states.

Answer: D

Explanation: Federalists wanted a strong central government while anti-federalists wanted a small government. Option D is a statement that would be made by an anti-federalist as it indicates the federal government had too much power.

QUESTION 6

Following the ratification of the Constitution of the United States, which of the following actions best displays that the Constitution would not become a new monarch?

    A. The inclusion of the Bill of Rights.

    B. George Washington stepping down after two terms as President.

    C. Vermont being admitted as the 14th State of the United States.

    D. Congress amending the method of electing the President.

Answer: B

Explanation: George Washington not seeking a third term as the President displayed the strongest evidence that the Constitution was not a new monarch. The people had the voice to elect individuals to the highest office of the land.

QUESTION 7

I.   explore the Missouri River

II. take observations of latitude & longitude, courses of the river, variations of the compass

III. observe the soil & face of the country

The above best represents which of the following?

A. Thomas Jefferson's instructions to Lewis and Clark
B. agreement with France for Louisiana Territory
C. exploration of oil and gas offshore in the Gulf of Mexico
D. Missouri Compromise of 1819

Answer: A

Explanation: Shortly after acquiring the Louisiana Territory from France, President Thomas Jefferson sent Meriwether Lewis and William Clark to explore the territory. President Thomas Jefferson instructions included to explore the Missouri River, to take observations of latitude & longitude, courses of the river, variations of the compass, and to observe the soil & face of the country.

QUESTION 8

Which of the following was the main reason British started to tax colonists?

A. to start building roads
B. to start community services
C. to pay the debt of the war
D. to gain money for government jobs

Answer: C

Explanation: The French and Indian War caused a significant amount of debt, which resulted in the British to start taxing colonists.

QUESTION 9

The formation of the Republican Party came as a direct passage of which of the following?

    A. Kansas-Nebraska Act

    B. Intolerable Act

    C. the Constitution

    D. the Articles of Confederation

Answer: A

Explanation: The Republican Party was established in 1854, and the Kansas-Nebraska Act was passed on May 30th, 1854.

QUESTION 10

In the Dred Scott decision of 1857, which act of Congress was declared unconstitutional by the United States Supreme Court?

    A. Fugitive Slave Law

    B. Kansas-Nebraska Act

    C. Missouri Compromise

    D. Commerce Compromise

Answer: C

Explanation: The Court ruled that Scott's brief residence outside Missouri did not bring about his emancipation under the Missouri Compromise, which the court ruled unconstitutional as it would "improperly deprive Scott's owner of his legal property."

QUESTION 11

Which of the following was NOT a direct cause of the Great Depression?

    A. Bank failure resulted in the loss of uninsured savings.

    B. The American economic policy with Europe.

    C. The stock market crashed on Black Tuesday.

    D. The aftermath of World War II.

Answer: D

Explanation: The Great Depression occurred before World War II, which actually helped end the Great Depression because it created jobs.

QUESTION 12

The black line in the image above best represents which of the following?

    A. Three-Fifth Compromise

    B. Kansas-Nebraska Act

    C. Missouri Compromise

    D. Commerce Compromise

Answer: C

Explanation: The Missouri Compromise prohibited slavery north of the 36°30' parallel, which is represented by the black line in the image.

QUESTION 13

Which country was NOT a part of the Triple Alliance?

- A. Germany
- B. Italy
- C. Russia
- D. Austria-Hungary

Answer: C

Explanation: Triple Alliance - Germany, Austria-Hungary, and Italy - stood against the three nations of the Triple Entente - France, Russia, and Great Britain.

QUESTION 14

Which of the following best describes the concentration of the Second New Deal?

- A. relief, recovery, and reform
- B. relief and recovery
- C. recovery and reform
- D. relief and reform

Answer: D

Explanation: The First New Deal focused on relief, recovery, and reform. With most of the recovery addressed in the First New Deal, the Second New Deal was focused on relief and reform.

QUESTION 15

Which of the following is the long term consequence of the Great Depression?

    A. unemployment

    B. poverty

    C. rise of fascism

    D. deterioration in education systems

Answer: C

Explanation: The Great Depression caused mass unemployment, poverty, and misery around the world. The long term consequence was the rise of fascism, which would present the greatest threat to human rights and world peace in the interwar years.

QUESTION 16

    I.   the fall of Poland

    II.   Lend-Lease Act

   III.   British forces leave Western Europe

   IV.   Allies stranded at Dunkirk

Of the above, which of the following are the causes of World War II?

    A. I and IV

    B. II and IV

    C. I and III

    D. III and IV

Answer: B

Explanation: Causes of World War II included allies stranded at Dunkirk and Lend-Lease Act. The effects were the fall of Poland and British forces leaving Western Europe.

QUESTION 17

I.   Donald Trump

II.   Herbert Hoover

III.   Dwight Eisenhower

IV.   Zachary Taylor

Which two presidents had neither prior military nor political experiences?

    A. I and II
    B. I and III
    C. I and IV
    D. III and IV

Answer: A

Explanation: Presidents Dwight Eisenhower and Zachary Taylor had military experiences. President Trump and President Hoover had neither political nor military experiences.

QUESTION 18

Which of the following best describes the difference between the League of Nations and the United Nations?

    A. League of Nations did not have members from several of the world's most important industrialized nations.
    B. League of Nations had the authority to enforce decisions made by the World Court.
    C. League of Nations could pass a resolution to intervene in any war.
    D. League of Nations focused on improving world health standards and providing aid to countries involved in wars.

Answer: A

Explanation: The correct answer is Option A. The League of Nations and the United Nations' difference is that the League of Nations did not have members from several of the world's most important industrialized nations.

QUESTION 19

Which of the following civil rights activists is most closely associated with the first large-scale United States demonstration against segregation?

A. Rosa Parks
B. Malcolm X
C. Harriet Tubman
D. Emily Dickenson

Answer: A

Explanation: Montgomery Bus Boycott was regarded as the first large-scale U.S. demonstration against segregation. Rosa Parks was a civil rights activist best known for her pivotal role in the Montgomery Bus Boycott.

QUESTION 20

When designing the American government, the framers of the Constitution

A. wanted a strong central government.
B. rejected the British constitutional tradition.
C. preferred the French constitution than the British constitution.
D. wanted all power to be distrusted to the colonies.

Answer: B

Explanation: The framers of the Constitution did not want anything to do with the ideas of the British.

QUESTION 21

Which of the following was the first to display the concept of supremacy of law over public officials?

- A. Magna Carta
- B. Common Sense
- C. Declaration of Independence
- D. Emancipation Proclamation

Answer: A

Explanation: Magna Carta was a charter of rights agreed to by King John of England at Runnymede. Magna Carta established for the first time the principle that everybody, including the king, was subject to the law. It was the first document to display the concept of supremacy of law over public officials.

QUESTION 22

Under the Federal System of Government, which of the following can be done by the state government and not the federal government?

- A. set up schools
- B. set up a postal service
- C. can collect taxes
- D. borrow money

Answer: A

Explanation: The federal government can set up an army and navy, issue money, set up a postal service, and control trade between states. A state government can set up schools, organize local government, run elections, and control trade within the state. Both governments can collect taxes, pass laws, set up courts, and borrow money.

QUESTION 23

Which of the following amendment does NOT deal with voting?

A. 15th Amendment
B. 16th Amendment
C. 23rd Amendment
D. 46th Amendment

Answer: B

Explanation: The 16th Amendment states that Congress shall have the power to lay and collect taxes on incomes, from whatever source derived, without apportionment among the several States, and without regard to any census or enumeration.

QUESTION 24

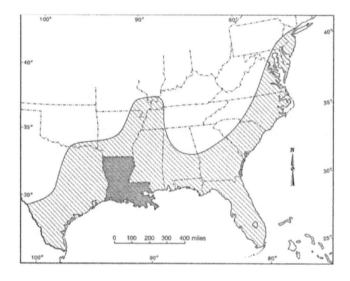

In the above image, what is indicated by the dash lines?

A. Coastal Plain
B. Appalachian Highlands
C. Canadian Shield
D. Interior Lowlands

Answer: A

Explanation: Coastal Plain region is located along the Atlantic Ocean and the Gulf of Mexico. The image indicates the Coastal Plain.

QUESTION 25

During the 20th century, there were fewer farms and fewer framers due to which of the following?

- A. advancement in technology
- B. expansion of the internet
- C. expansion of formal education system
- D. decrease in population in rural areas

Answer: A

Explanation: During the 20th century, the population grew to require more need for feeding people. There were fewer but larger farms. In addition, fewer individuals identified themselves as framers. Large conglomerates ran most farms using advanced technologies.

QUESTION 26

In the above image, the dash line area indicates which of the following?

- A. Great Plains
- B. Interior Lowlands
- C. Basin and Range
- D. Coastal Range

Answer: C

Explanation: Basin and Range geographic region are located west of the Rocky Mountains and east of the Sierra Nevada, which is indicated in the image.

QUESTION 27

Which of the following should be placed in the blank box in the image above?

   A. China
   B. Kashmir
   C. Nepal
   D. Bangladesh

Answer: B

Explanation: Kashmir is the disputed region between Pakistan and India. Kashmir is the northernmost geographical region of the Indian subcontinent.

QUESTION 28

Movement of massive glaciers through the mid-continent, a process that began about one million years ago during the Pleistocene Epoch, resulted in what is known today as _____.

    A. Helena Mountains
    B. Great Lakes
    C. Arctic Blast
    D. Greenland

Answer: B

Explanation: Movement of massive glaciers through the mid-continent, a process that began about one million years ago during the Pleistocene Epoch, resulted in what is known today as Great Lakes.

Pacific – 3:00 ; Mountain – 4:00; Central – 5:00; Eastern – 6:00

A flight leaves Houston, Texas, at 2:00 PM for Riverside, California. The duration of the flight is four and one-half hours. According to the map above, what will be the local time in Riverside when the flight lands?

    A. 1:30 PM
    B. 4:30 PM
    C. 6:30 PM
    D. 7:30 PM

Answer: B

Explanation: The flight leaves 2:00 PM Central time zone, and the flight is 4 ½ hours. From the Central time zone standpoint, the flight will arrive in Riverside at 6:30 PM. In Riverside, the time will be 4:30 PM as it is 2 hours behind the Central time zone.

QUESTION 30

Madison is writing a report about life in modern Pakistan. His teacher asked him to use a primary source and two secondary sources. Which resource could Madison use as a primary source?

    A. the diary of a Pakistani poet
    B. an encyclopedia article about Pakistan
    C. a chapter about Pakistan from his history book
    D. a timeline showing major events in Pakistan history

Answer: A

Explanation: The only option that provides a firsthand account of life in modern Pakistan is a diary of a Pakistani poet. All other options are secondary sources.

QUESTION 31

What is the name of the imaginary line that divides the Earth into Northern and Southern Hemispheres?

    A. latitude
    B. longitude
    C. equator
    D. prime meridian

Answer: C

Explanation: The equator, or line of 0 degrees latitude, divides the Earth into the Northern and Southern hemispheres.

QUESTION 32

    I.   The equator is a line of latitude.

    II.   The prime meridian is a line of longitude.

    III.   The equator is an imaginary line at 0-degree longitude.

Of the above, which of the statements are accurately written?

    A. I, II, and III
    B. I and II
    C. I and III
    D. II and III

Answer: B

Explanation: The prime meridian is an imaginary line at 0-degree longitude.

QUESTION 33

Which of the following determines a person's job, social group, and marriage?

    A. caste system
    B. hierarchy system
    C. marriage status
    D. societies norm status

Answer: A

Explanation: A caste is a form of social stratification characterized by endogamy, hereditary transmission of a lifestyle. This includes occupation, status in a hierarchy, customary social interaction, and exclusion.

QUESTION 34

Which of the following best indicates the earliest to latest use of renewable energy resources?

    A. wood – fossil fuels – hydropower – biofuels
    B. fossil fuels – wood – hydropower – biofuels
    C. wood – fossil fuels – biofuels – hydropower
    D. hydropower – biofuels – fossil fuels – wood

Answer: B

Explanation: The question is asking for the earliest use to the latest use of renewable energy. Until the mid-1800s, wood was the source of energy for heating, cooking, and light. From the late 1800s until today, fossil fuels have been the major sources of energy. Hydropower and solid biomass were widely used until the 1990s. Since then, biofuels, solar, and wind energy have increased.

QUESTION 35

Of the following, which best explains how deviance helps strengthen conformity in society?

    A. It requires no need for agents of social control.
    B. Establishes boundaries between right and wrong.
    C. Establishes punishment for wrongful acts.
    D. It requires people to follow the rules of society.

Answer: B

Explanation: Deviance means departing from usual or accepted standards. By indicating what is considered deviance, society is taking steps to suppress those behaviors. Society is establishing the boundaries between right and wrong.

QUESTION 36

Which of the following societies had the greatest impact on modern democratic societies?

A. Ancient Roman
B. Ancient Athens
C. Roman Republic
D. Byzantine Empire

Answer: B

Explanation: Athenians were the first to practice direct democracy in which every citizen could vote. This resembles the modern democratic societies, having the right to vote.

QUESTION 37

All of the following contributed to the War of 1812 except:

A. The British navy's practice of removing sailors from American merchant ships.
B. Many in Britain thought that Presidents Jefferson and Madison were pro-French and anti-British.
C. The American perception that Britain did not recognize her as a fully independent nation.
D. Britain had been fighting the United States, more or less, since 1793.

Answer: D

Explanation: Option D is incorrectly written. Britain had been fighting France, more or less, since 1793.

QUESTION 38

If California experiences a year-long drought, a significant negative effect can be on which of the following?

A. fruit production
B. population patterns
C. tourism
D. employment

Answer: A

Explanation: California produces a sizable majority of American fruits, vegetables, and nuts. To have a year-long drought will have a negative effect on fruit production. Other options can see the impact, but the most significant will be on fruit production.

QUESTION 39

Which of the following countries is currently at the most economic risk due to a reduction in petroleum resources?

A. Iran
B. Iraq
C. Mexico
D. Venezuela

Answer: C

Explanation: Of the choices, Mexico is the only non-OPEC country. OPEC has the majority of the world's proven oil reserves.

QUESTION 40

Jimmy asked the bank to give him $10,000. By the time the loan is repaid, Jimmy has paid the bank $10,600. What does the additional $600 represent?

A. interest
B. investment
C. fees
D. inflation rate

Answer: A

Explanation: The additional amount of accounts for the interest rate that is incurred for borrowing money. Option C can be confused for the answer, but fees are typically not $600.

QUESTON 41

Country X has no domestic sources of wood; it imports all wood from wood-producing countries. If the price of wood in wood-producing countries rises substantially, which of the following is most likely to occur?

A. Country X will see a quick decline in home construction.
B. Country X will import more woods to meet rising demand.
C. Country X will use an alternative material to construct homes.
D. Country X will see an increase in housing prices.

Answer: D

Explanation: Wood is a common material to construct homes. If the price of wood increases, the prices of homes will increase. Option A is incorrect because nothing suggests a quick decline in home construction.

QUESTION 42

Kelly has decided to give up her part-time job to return to school. Which of the following is one potential economic risk Kelly is accepting?

    A. the loss of income from giving up her part-time job
    B. possibility of not getting a job in the field, Kelly has decided to go back to school for
    C. not finding another part-time job in the future
    D. the increase in expenses due to going back to school

Answer: B

Explanation: Risk is the possibility of losing something of value. Risk is unknown when making a decision. Options A and D are known factors. Option C is not a risk associated with Kelly's decision. Option B is a real risk that is a part of her decision and can have an economic impact on Kelly.

QUESTION 43

Which of the following best illustrates the meaning of the economic term scarcity?

    A. individuals unable to buy basic household items
    B. businesses lack funds to invest in making a profit
    C. employees lack of training to gain career advances
    D. manufactures lack raw materials necessary to fulfill demand

Answer: D

Explanation: In economics, scarcity is concerning a problem having to do with raw materials limited by nature. Raw materials can be limited or scarce.

QUESTION 44

Monopoly is best characterized as

A. strong control over price.
B. strong control over items.
C. rarely influenced by government.
D. few barriers to reach the market.

Answer: A

Explanation: In a monopoly, companies control the available supply, so they can raise prices without losing consumers. If there is no competition for the supply, individuals can increase the price.

QUESTION 45

The above form of writing belongs to which ancient civilization?

A. Sumerian
B. Egyptian
C. Greek
D. Hebrew

Answer: C

Explanation: The Greek alphabet has been used to write the Greek language since the late ninth or early eighth century BC. The above image shows writing belonging to Greeks.

QUESTION 46

Columbia grows coffee efficiently and effectively, and coffee is the country's largest agricultural product. Columbia also has an automobile industry that is unable to efficiently manufacture automobiles. The United States efficiently manufactures automobiles; however, the country grows a small amount of coffee in Utah. Columbia's economy is ranked below 10th in the world, while the United States has the largest economy. Based on the information, which statement best explains why Columbia would want to trade with the United States?

    A. Columbia has a comparative advantage in growing coffee over the United States.
    B. Columbia needs more cars in the streets for transportation to support the coffee business.
    C. Columbia has a comparative advantage in the technological advantage in the manufacturing of automobiles over the United States.
    D. Columbia needs to sell coffee to the United States, or Columbia's economy will not sustain.

Answer: A

Explanation: Columbia has a comparative advantage in growing of coffee over the United States. Columbia grows coffee with a lower opportunity cost than the United States. This allows Columbia to have a comparative advantage over the United States.

QUESTION 47

In a market economy, if the price of an item increases, the quantity demand by buyers and quantity supplied by producers will change in which of the following ways?

Quantity Demanded Quantity	Supplied by Consumers by Producers
A. decrease	increase
B. decrease	decrease
C. increase	increase
D. increase	decrease

Answer: A

Explanation: Fewer consumers will want to buy the good as the price increases; most people do not like spending a lot of money. Producers will provide more of the good in anticipation of making increased profits.

QUESTION 48

What is the impact on the United States with increased oil usage around the world?

    A. Individuals pay more for gasoline.
    B. Energy sales remain the same.
    C. Energy cost declines.
    D. Individuals' need for gasoline decreases.

Answer: A

Explanation: If there is more usage of oil, the price will increase. People will always need gasoline to drive, so people will pay more for gasoline.

QUESTION 49

Which of the following organization is responsible for the promotion of consumer protection and the elimination and prevention of anticompetitive business practices?

    A. Federal Reserve Bank
    B. Federal Trade Commission
    C. Consumer Protection Agency
    D. United States Commerce Department

Answer: B

Explanation: The Federal Trade Commission is responsible for the promotion of consumer protection and the elimination and prevention of anticompetitive business practices.

QUESTION 50

In 2018, California had 53 representatives in the United States House of Representatives while Louisiana had 6 representatives. What accounts for the differences in these numbers?

A. land area of the states
B. population of the states
C. wealth within the states
D. number of counties within the states

Answer: B

Explanation: The more population in the state the more representatives in the United States House of Representatives. California's population is significantly higher than Louisiana's population.

QUESTION 51

Which of the following best describes the idea of manifest destiny?

A. slavery should be allowed in the East
B. all individuals had the right to freedom
C. preventing European colonies from entering into the Americas
D. the United States had the right to expand to the Pacific Ocean

Answer: D

Explanation: Manifest destiny was the 19th-century doctrine that the expansion of the United States throughout the American continents was both justified and necessary.

QUESTION 52

Which of the following is an example of a factor of production?

    A. supply
    B. demand
    C. development
    D. entrepreneurship

Answer: D

Explanation: Factor of production include land, labor, capital, and entrepreneurship.

QUESTION 53

    I.   high population growth rate/size
   II.   high rates of unemployment
  III.   high per capita real income

Of the above, which of the following accurately characterizes developing countries?

    A. I and II
    B. I and III
    C. II and III
    D. I, II, and III

Answer: A

Explanation: Common characteristic of developing countries is that they either have high population growth rates or large populations. In rural areas, unemployment suffers from large seasonal variations. Low per capita real income is one of the main characteristics of developing economies.

QUESTION 54

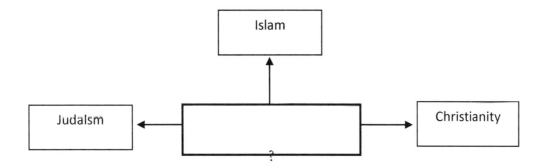

Which of the following best completes the web?

    A. acknowledge the existence of Jesus
    B. use of the same holy book
    C. holy city of Mecca
    D. karma

Answer: A

Explanation: In Christianity, Jesus is believed to be the Son of God and the second Person of the Holy Trinity. Jews believe Jesus of Nazareth did not fulfill messianic prophecies. In Islam, Jesus is the prophet and messenger of God. All three religions acknowledge the existence of Jesus.

QUESTION 55

What was the main reason why Phoenicians establish dozens of colonies along the Mediterranean coast?

    A. to make money
    B. to protect their main cities from invaders
    C. to improve and expand trade
    D. to attract new members to their civilization

Answer: C

Explanation: Phoenicians establish dozens of colonies along the Mediterranean coast to improve and expand on trade.

QUESTION 56

Which of the following best displays the action of a good citizen?

    A. joining a library club

    B. throwing away litter

    C. buying a new house

    D. making a dinner

Answer: B

Explanation: Good citizens are those helping to better society and communities, and throwing away litter is a good example of an action by a good citizen.

QUESTION 57

Population and Square Miles of Countries

Country	Land in square miles	Population in millions
Egypt	6500	5.5
Iraq	172344	20.2
Jordan	35343	3.8
Iran	163234	18.5

According to the above data, which country is the most densely populated?

    A. Egypt

    B. Iraq

    C. Jordan

    D. Iran

Answer: A

Explanation: The population density is equal to the number of people divided by the land area. Using this formula, the population density of Egypt is about 846 people/miles. Another approach is to round all the numbers and divide, and the answer will be Egypt as the most densely populated region.

QUESTION 58

Which of the following is a finished product?

  A. laptop
  B. horse
  C. plant
  D. mountain

Answer: A

Explanation: Finished goods are goods that have completed the manufacturing process. Of the choices, laptop is a finished product.

QUESTION 59

Flake wrote a school article about six goods produced in China and sold to other countries. What is the best title for Flake's report?

  A. Jobs in China
  B. Exports of China
  C. Items in China
  D. Buyers in China

Answer: B

Explanation: The article is about goods being exported to other countries, so the best title is "Exports of China."

QUESTION 60

Which region is usually hot, very dry, and has few trees?

  A. arctic
  B. grassland
  C. rain forest
  D. desert

Answer: D

Explanation: Desert is very hot, very dry, and has few little trees.

This page is intentionally left blank.

By: LQ Publications

This page is intentionally left blank.

CPSIA information can be obtained
at www.ICGtesting.com
Printed in the USA
BVHW011300070421
604422BV00013B/215